Homemade
NATURAL
HAIR CARE

·········· with ··········

Essential Oils

'A conscious approach to health & wellness'

carmabooks.com

You are invited to to join our **Free Book Club** *mailing list. Sign up via our website to receive* **special offers** *and* **free for a limited time** *Health & Wellness eBooks!*

Homemade
NATURAL
HAIR CARE
············ with ··········
Essential Oils

DIY RECIPES to Promote Hair Growth, Shine + Repair

Carmen Reeves

Disclaimer

This book provides general information, experiences and extensive research regarding health and related subjects. The information provided in this book, and in any linked materials, are not intended to be construed as medical advice. There are no 'typical' results from the information provided - as individuals differ, the results will differ. If the reader or any other person has a medical concern, he or she should consult with an appropriately licensed physician or health care worker. Never disregard professional medical advice or delay in seeking it because of something you have read in this book or in any linked materials.

Carma Books
carmabooks.com

hello@carmabooks.com

CONTENTS

CHAPTER 2: Nourishing Organic Care for Normal Hair

CHAPTER 3: Products for Dry and Brittle Hair

INTRODUCTION

Thank you and congratulations on your purchase of *'Homemade Natural Hair Care (with Essential Oils)'*. This book will be your guide to improving and restoring your hair's overall health, condition, growth and appearance.

You are probably sick and tired of the amount of toxins we are all bombarded with when buying cosmetic products and dissatisfied with the many commercial store-bought products you have tried and tested. Most of these products are loaded with chemicals and harsh ingredients, which over time, can result in a variety of skin and hair issues. At first, the damaging effects of chemical-laden products can go unnoticed as we become mesmerized by the synthetic smells and texture that commercial products leave in our hair. However, over time we realize that this sensory allure is merely a short-term fix and our hair begins to suffer – becoming dull, lifeless, dry and brittle; and causing hair loss, dandruff and breakage.

You may already be familiar with my deep interest in natural living and organic beauty products. I have received such wonderful feedback from the many people who tried the recipes in my *Homemade Organic Skin & Body Care* book, claiming how effective such a pure way of treating your body can be. If you're beginning your natural beauty journey from this book, you will surely be persuaded to continue using homemade products after you see your hair looking shinier and healthier each week. Your hair (and mind and body!) will thank you.

Why You Should Use Homemade Products for Your Hair

A Cost-effective, Creative and Proven Alternative

Homemade hair care offers you a guarantee that you cannot find in purchasing commercial products. Although many products are marketed as 'natural' in stores and online, they often come with a high price tag or unnecessary hidden ingredients and fillers. Much like preparing a home-cooked meal, there is nothing safer or more satisfying than hand-making your very own shampoo and conditioner with ingredients you may already have in your pantry, fridge and/or garden.

More and more people have delved into making their own hair care products for great reason. The ingredients used contain wonderful benefits and the creative preparation process, like a craft with therapeutic effects, is enjoyable. The aromatic properties of essential oils are used for many health and wellness purposes and more people are beginning to integrate them into their lifestyle through various means, including hair and body care.

Practical and Flexible Freedom of Choice

Imagine the pleasure and independence you will have when you make your own hair care products – you are able to decide on every ingredient used, with specialized recipes tailored to your specific problem or hair type. Consider what it really means to have no unknown and harmful substances in your shampoo or conditioner. The end result will be 100% organic and you'll have the opportunity to be creative and ingenious with your products. Feel free to experiment with new combinations; you can carefully decide on ingredients – essential oils and other raw materials – you should use according to what you already know works for you. Creating hair care products at home can become a real hobby for many people, and the results: totally worth it!

Put a Stop to the Sea of Toxins (and Keep Healthy!)

With homemade hair care products, you will avoid the many dreaded toxins and detergents inevitably present in synthetic alternatives and your hair will reap the benefits of a much more soothing and gentle treatment. Homemade shampoos will cleanse your hair just as well as any other chemical-laden shampoos without irritating your scalp or stripping away natural sebum – essential in nourishing the hair from its root.

Do note that other lifestyle choices can have an impact on your hair's health in conjunction with these organic body care recipes. For instance, it has been shown that a diet rich in plant-based foods (a colorful rainbow of fruits and vegetables), maintaining *healthy gut balance, ample exercise, plenty of water, and keeping nutritional deficiencies and hormonal balance in check can positively contribute to beautiful, healthy hair.*

An Easily Available Hair Care Solution

Homemade hair care is suitable for anyone, even for those who don't want to create complicated mixtures or purchase many new products. For instance, you can use ingredients you might already have in your own kitchen and/or garden, whilst only purchasing a couple of essential oil varieties with which you can experiment. Many people find simple solutions for their hair using olive oil, avocado or herbal infusions. Essential oils mixed and diluted with oils and other plant-based elements are fantastic for a multitude of uses. Read on to discover the myriad of benefits you'll receive when you choose to create the cruelty-free essential oils formulas presented in this book.

What Essential Oils Can Do for Your Hair

You are probably wondering, *'Why use essential oils?'* *in your shampoo or conditioner. 'Will my hair get too greasy?'* and *'What if I already have oily hair?'*

The Optimal Nourishing Formula for Your Scalp and Hair Growth

First of all, essential oils are very concentrated – you can find potent versions of many plants or fruits in the form of an essential oil. Secondly, they contain an amazingly high level of antioxidants that you can obtain by using them in your homemade products. The beneficial properties in essential oils make your hair shiny, silky, and more vibrantly healthy; plus, the rich antioxidant content helps boosts hair growth and hair repair processes, which may encourage you to discard any useless, synthetic serums.

Essential oils do not negatively affect your scalp or sebum, particularly when used in conjunction with the right companion ingredients. In fact, some people may already have an imbalance of natural oils due to past use of various styling products. Essential oil will help regulate your hair's natural oil production by replenishing your scalp and, additionally, nourishing your hair from root to tip. Essential oils are very easily absorbed, deeply penetrate the hair follicle and nourish it to the core. Artificial products you can find in stores often contain a composition that doesn't allow any 'good' ingredients to be properly absorbed by your hair – a cocktail of synthetic elements that often keeps the product sticking to the surface of the hair shaft.

Exhilarating Aromatherapy for Your Wellbeing

Last, but not least, essential oils evoke an enticing feast for your senses. Aromatherapy is an added advantage in using essential oils in your homemade hair care. Not only will your hair regenerate and become healthier, you will also revel in a vigorous wellness experience. Being surrounded by the powerful aroma of essential oils will positively affect your state of mind, and at the same time, the aromatherapy can be used for mindfulness: the intense scents will activate your senses and compel you to yield completely to the present moment.

How to Use Essential Oils

Due to their high potency and concentration, it is important to use essential oils correctly and sparingly by remembering to dilute with carrier oils or other plant-based ingredients. Some common carrier oil types that are affordable and easy to find include: *olive oil, sunflower oil, coconut oil, almond oil, castor oil, jojoba oil and avocado oil.* Choose your favorite carrier oil to dilute the essential oils of your choice and you'll be amazed at the powerful cumulative effect and added benefits they will have on your hair.

As a general rule, every 1 drop of essential oil should be diluted with at least 5ml of carrier oil or other fluid (with the exception of a few essential oils that can be used 'neat' or direct onto the skin, such as lavender or tea tree).

Note: Do not ingest essential oils and keep out of reach of children and pets. Ensure essential oils do not come into contact with your eyes and use with caution if you are pregnant, planning to become pregnant or have any pre-existing medical conditions. If you have any sensitivities or concerns about any of the ingredients in this book, ensure you try a patch test first.

Choosing Cruelty-free Ingredients is a Conscious Choice

There Are Cruelty-free Alternatives for Practically Anything

One of the key components of the recipes in this book is the use of vegan and cruelty-free ingredients to ensure none of our furry friends are exploited or harmed in the pursuit of beauty. In case you are accustomed to several ingredients that are of an animal origin (such as: honey, eggs or yoghurt), rest assured you can always find alternative substitutes with comparable and even more effective benefits (such as moisturizing coconut milk, nutrient packed maple syrup and antioxidant-rich fresh fruits), as outlined throughout this book.

The 'Green' Ethical Choice

The most important aspects of choosing cruelty-free ingredients for hair care are for ethical and environmental reasons. Did you know that every person who adopts a cruelty-free lifestyle (through means of diet, apparel and cosmetics) saves more than 100 animals per year? It's amazing to think that our small, day-to-day choices could save the lives of countless beautiful animals. The production and processing of animal ingredients also place an added impact of stress on our environment. By making conscious choices, you are contributing to a 'green' lifestyle for the improvement and good of our earth and all those inhabiting it.

CHAPTER 1

The Art of Making Shampoo and Conditioner at Home

How Easy Is It?

This chapter will prepare you for the art of homemade hair care. It will guide you through a few steps that you need in order to make your own shampoo and conditioner; plus, you can also use some of these hints to enhance your other homemade hair and body products, including: masks, soaps, lotions and potions. You may be wondering whether your time will be compromised when creating your own products at home, but fear not: preparation is simple! Neither your wallet nor your schedule will suffer from your wise decision to treat your hair with kindness.

Easy and Familiar with a Twist

Creating your own shampoo or conditioner is not much more complicated than preparing masks. Many of us may have already experimented with face or hair masks in past by using the ingredients in our homes – just explore your pantry to discover what you can utilize. You will have to purchase very few additional items for your organic hair care, namely, the essential oils you choose to use. Start by using products you are familiar with for their nourishing properties. You will feel more 'at home' with your ingredients and you'll already have great confidence in the efficiency of your hair care. So, what can you spot right now in your pantry? Coconut milk? Oranges? Maple syrup? Avocado? Olive oil? Sage? Once you have your essential oils, you're almost there.

Homemade Hair Care is Quick and Versatile

Some people are already familiar with making various cosmetic products, including soaps, body butters and scrubs, lip balms; and even lotions and perfumes. Luckily, shampoo is one of the easiest things to prepare at home – you only have to know the basics and be aware of a few simple combination rules. You should also be mindful of some of the essential properties each ingredient contains in order to use it creatively in a variety of other products, too. The rest is pure pleasure, as you will discover in the following chapters.

What You Need

The Right Cleansing Agent and Container

You will need several ingredients and a good container to store your formulas. You may reuse and recycle an empty, cleaned shampoo bottle or you can also purchase a squeezable plastic bottle from your nearest dollar shop or variety store. Alternatively, you can also place the formula in a glass jar; however, I recommend using a squeezable container, which makes for easier use whilst you are washing your hair.

So, what else do you need for your shampoo? Just a few simple ingredients:

- *A cleansing agent* (*as outlined below*)
- *Nourishing ingredients of your choice* (*essential oils, herbal infusions, fresh fruits, etc.*)
- *Organic flour* (*optional, and works best for oily hair–corn, rice or arrowroot flour work well*)
- *Carrier oil of your choice* (*quantity depends on the amount of hydration you desire*)

You have various options when it comes to your cleansing agent:

Some people use **potassium hydroxide,** otherwise known as 'caustic potash' – a water-soluble compound, a pH adjuster and a versatile cleaning agent – similar in chemical structure to 'lye'. The process of creating liquid soap with potassium hydroxide involves dissolving the agent in water and mixing it with a very consistent, but nourishing ingredient, like warmed up coconut oil, whilst taking extreme caution not to let this powerful cleaning agent come into direct skin contact (you *must* wear gloves and/or a filter mask, as it can be corrosive to the skin in its pure form). Some people choose not to use potassium hydroxide for this very reason – the method is slightly more laborious and the compound, even after dilution, may cause some irritation for those with extremely sensitive skin. You may, of course, choose this option if you have no known sensitivities and have some extra time on your hands, as some people enjoy the process. The process involves boiling and mixing everything together until you get a smooth, consistent paste. This will act as the base for your shampoo. You can then combine it with your chosen nourishing and therapeutic ingredients.

If you want something gentler or prefer to use purer ingredients, another solution to making your shampoo is **baking soda**, which you may conveniently already have in your pantry at home. Baking soda is a gentle, alkaline ingredient that effectively removes dirt and chemical build-up in your hair. It is mild, yet still powerful enough to cleanse impurities and give your hair extra volume and shine.

Other people have found great results with the effects of **apple cider vinegar**. This all-natural ingredient acts as a mild acidic base that can regulate the pH balance of your hair. Use quality, organic vinegar for best results and extra shine. This option is especially recommended for those with oily or tangled hair due to over-styling or having long or curly locks. Apple cider vinegar is just as effective as baking soda, so feel free to try them both to see which option works best for your hair type. You should use one tablespoon of baking soda or apple cider vinegar per one cup of water as a general ratio when preparing your shampoo. Adjust quantities as desired.

Another simple cleansing agent alternative is liquid soap. **Liquid Castile Soap**, made from 100% plant-based oils (typically olive or coconut oil), is praised as a gentle yet effective cleansing base for shampoo, particularly for those who enjoy a slight foaming effect. This cleansing agent is gentle on the skin making it perfect for those with a dry or sensitive scalp. A little goes a long way.

Extra Nutrition Through Herbs and Plants

Although essential oils contain a concentrated quantity of nutrients from the plant or fruit they were extracted from, you may add further nourishment to your shampoo (or other hair care products) by means of **raw, natural herbs**. Just like preparing a tea, you can boil and brew the plants of your choice and use this nutritive, aromatic liquid in your formula.

Baking soda, apple cider vinegar, or liquid Castile soap will cleanse your hair; essential oils and carrier oils will *deeply hydrate and nourish your hair*; and added herbs, plants or fruits will *provide additional nutrients to the hair and scalp*. The perfect combination for healthful hair care, not to mention a pleasure for your senses!

And what about conditioner? Much like creating shampoo, you will need nourishing plant ingredients and oils of your choice, plus a toning, yet very mild agent such as vinegar or lemon juice. Use essential oils and carrier oils in moderate quantities, dependent on how oily or dry your hair is.

So now that you know how easy and enjoyable it is to make your own natural hair products, let's move on to see exactly what ingredients and quantities you need for certain hair types.

CHAPTER 2

Nourishing Organic Care for Normal Hair

It's time to master the many recipes that will become your secret weapon in combating hair damage and enhancing natural beauty and shine. If you feel exceptionally creative and imaginative, feel free to alter the recipe to suit your desired results. I have however discovered the value in the following combinations, which I am delighted to share with you. You can use these 'normal' hair recipes for practically any hair type.

Shampoo and Conditioner

Stimulating Carrot Seed Oil Shampoo

Ingredients:
- Water (1 cup)
- Maple Syrup (2 tablespoons)
- Carrot Seed Essential Oil (5-10 drops)
- Jojoba Oil (10 drops)
- Liquid Castile Soap (1/3 cup) or cleansing agent of choice

Directions:

Combine all ingredients together into a consistent mixture, shake well, and wash your hair with desired quantity. Rinse well and apply your conditioner of choice afterwards. Use shampoo within one month. Best stored in refrigerator.

Benefits:

This shampoo is particularly beneficial for dry hair or dandruff, giving a vitamin boost from the carrot seed oil. Carrot seed oil is purifying, detoxifying, and stimulating with a mild aroma. It improves your circulation, stimulates growth, strengthens your hair, and aids in any scalp dryness. Jojoba oil dilutes the carrot seed essential oil and adds extra hydration to the formula. Its structure resembles our natural sebum, which adds elasticity and is not greasy. Maple syrup is soothing and deeply nourishing with wonderful antibacterial properties. Your shampoo will have a warm, energizing sensation.

Nutritious and Aromatic
Orange Oil Shampoo

Ingredients:

- Coconut Milk (1/3 cup)
- Liquid Castile Soap (½ cup)
- Orange Essential Oil (10 drops)
- Castor Oil (10 drops)

Directions:

Add all ingredients into a container and shake well until all ingredients are combined. Lather and wash hair with desired quantity and rinse well. Use shampoo within one month. Best stored in refrigerator.

Benefits:

This shampoo is extremely nourishing due to coconut milk's high vitamin and mineral content, containing high levels of vitamin E, C, B1, B 3, B5, B6, calcium, magnesium, iron, and selenium. You can choose a particular coconut oil that is suitable for your hair; for example, you may use a thicker coconut milk for normal hair that contains about 20% fat. Coconut milk acts as a balm that nourishes hair intensively from root to tip and is beneficial for hair repair, preventing hair loss, detangling and hydrating, as well as stimulating hair growth. Orange oil is loaded with antioxidants and adds a fresh, enchanting fragrance that your senses will love. It nourishes the hair without feeling heavy or greasy. You will see your hair becoming thicker and stronger when using this shampoo regularly.

Repairing Herbal Conditioner with Lavender Oil

Ingredients:

- Water (1 cup)
- Herbs of choice (try nettle, sage, chamomile or nut-tree leaves)

- Lavender Oil (5 drops)
- Apple Cider Vinegar (1 tablespoon)
- Almond Oil (3 tablespoons)

Directions:

Boil water and pour over herbs, let steep for 20 minutes. Strain liquid and pour into a suitable container to be mixed with other ingredients. Add all ingredients and mix well. You can use this conditioner for several months if you store in a cool, dry place. Lather onto your hair (especially the ends) and leave in or gently rinse.

Benefits:

Vinegar is a traditional, yet potent remedy that fortifies and deeply cleanses the hair. This is an effective antibacterial ingredient that removes build-up, such as: dirt, oil or residual styling products.

Numerous herbs can stimulate hair growth and make the hair shaft stronger. Nettle may help bring back natural hues to graying hair. You can also use nut-tree leaves, recommended only if you have brown or dark hair, as the natural pigment may easily show in blonde hues (which of course works well if you choose to add darker shades into your hair). Chamomile is a great alternative for those with lighter hair. Nettle is a well-known and appreciated hair fortifier, as it stimulates hair growth and adds shine to dull, brittle hair. If you have balding problems, nettle is one of the best natural conditioner remedies that you can apply directly to your scalp. Sage is also an excellent treatment for hair loss and graying hair and will add extra shine and luster.

Almond oil is extremely moisturizing and stimulating with high levels of magnesium. If you have long or curly hair with split ends, you have found one of the best weapons to make your hair look smooth, glossy and healthy again. It works to help detangle hair with ease and avoid breakage. Use this soothing conditioner often if you have any kind of scalp inflammation or irritation.

Lavender oil is particularly calming and relaxing for both your hair and your mind. It releases stress and evokes a balancing and soothing effect no matter where it is applied.

Soothing Rosemary Oil and Lemon Hair Conditioner

Ingredients:
- Apple Cider Vinegar (1 cup)
- Rosemary Oil (10 drops)
- Lemon Juice (2-3 tablespoons)
- Sunflower Oil (1/3 cup)

Directions:
Mix all ingredients together into a container and shake well. Lather onto your hair, let sit for 5 minutes, and rinse thoroughly.

Benefits:
A great 'go to' conditioner when you need a quick and cost-effective solution to nourish your hair naturally.

Lemon will act as a unique tonic that will also add shine to your hair, whilst sunflower oil will provide nutrients and dilutes your rosemary essential oil. Ensure you use unrefined sunflower oil if you want to take advantage of its full benefits. Lemon juice contains vitamin C and antioxidants and adds a fresh, revitalizing fragrance to your conditioner. Rosemary essential oil is incredibly soothing for your scalp. Apply as a tonic (diluted with your preferred carrier oil) if you suffer from any irritation. Rosemary helps activate hair growth, because it dilates blood vessels and stimulates your follicles to produce new hair.

Hair Masks

Rejuvenating and Enticing Vanilla Oil Mask

Ingredients:
- Avocado (1 half)
- Vanilla Essential Oil (10 drops)
- Cherries (5-7, peeled and pitted)
- Water (½ cup)
- Herbs (choose your favorite)

Directions:

Boil water and steep herbs until cooled. Strain infused water and add all ingredients into your blender. Blitz until smooth. Evenly apply mixture to your hair and scalp and let sit for at least 15-20 minutes. Rinse well and gently towel dry.

Benefits:

This hair mask is amazingly moisturizing and replenishing due to the high vitamin and mineral content in avocado. Apart from providing your hair with natural Vitamin E, magnesium, potassium, and Vitamin B5, avocado will regulate the natural production of sebum. Cherries have a wonderful fragrance and are rich in vitamin C and antioxidants. Vanilla essential oil will add to the deeply moisturizing effect of avocado and will charm you with a lingering, exotic fragrance. Vanilla essential oil stimulates hair growth and it makes your hair super silky. This formula will boost circulation, tone and rejuvenate, and make your hair look and feel richer.

Nourishing Banana and Sandalwood Oil Hair Mask

Ingredients:

- Banana (1)
- Sandalwood Essential Oil (10 drops)
- Coconut Oil (1/4 cup)
- Water (½ cup)
- Herbs (chamomile or nettle)

Directions:

Boil water and prepare an infusion using the herbs of your choice, depending on your hair color and the condition of your scalp. Chamomile is suitable for blonde hair, promotes shine and alleviates irritation. Nettle is suitable for most hair colors, promotes growth and slightly darkens the hair. Blitz everything together in your blender until you achieve a creamy consistency. Evenly apply to your hair and let sit for at least 15-20 minutes. Rinse well and gently towel dry. Use this mask at least twice a week.

Benefits:

Banana regulates the production of oil, strengthens follicles and is a great source of potassium, vitamin C, B6, magnesium and zinc. It provides a consistent base for your mask and will deeply hydrate your hair. Sandalwood essential oil adds an irresistible fragrance to the formula, encouraging concentration and focus, and helps treat dry ends. Coconut oil makes the perfect conditioner for normal hair since it is moisturizing without leaving a greasy residue, leaving your hair lustrous and remarkably soft.

CHAPTER 3

Products for Dry and Brittle Hair

Dry hair may require more frequent treatments and conditioning to maintain a healthy feel. If your hair is also brittle, never fear – there are a few natural hair care solutions that will help you achieve gorgeous shine and luster.

Shampoo and Conditioner

Moisturizing Avocado and Orange Blossom Oil Shampoo

Ingredients:

- Apple Cider Vinegar (1 cup)
- Orange Blossom Essential Oil (5-7 drops)
- Avocado (1 half)
- Olive Oil (2-3 tablespoons)

Directions:

Mix vinegar with mashed avocado and add both oils. If you don't easily get a consistent paste, you can use your blender to make your formula creamy. Store shampoo in the fridge for 1-2 weeks and shake well before applying to your hair.

Benefits:

This shampoo recipe combines the captivating fragrance of orange blossom with the unique and nourishing ingredients of avocado to nourish your scalp and hair. Rich in vitamin E and B, it offers a reliable solution to stimulate and accelerate hair growth, whether you run the risk of hair loss, or you just want richer and healthier hair. The formula is easily absorbed into the hair shaft and is perfect for dry, split ends.

Orange blossom essential oil is ideal for regeneration and shine and by mixing with olive oil, becomes a highly hydrating combination for your scalp and hair. After regular use, your hair will feel strong and lustrous and those rebellious strands of hair will be 'tamed'.

Hydrating Aloe Vera, Glycerin, and Geranium Essential Oil Shampoo

Ingredients:

- Water (½ cup)
- Liquid Castile soap (½ cup)
- Aloe Vera Gel (1/3 cup)
- Glycerin (1 teaspoon)
- Almond Oil (2-3 teaspoons)
- Geranium Essential Oil (10 drops)

Directions:

Add all ingredients into a container and shake well until combined. Lather desired amount into hair, then rinse well. Use shampoo within one month.

Benefits:

This shampoo is extraordinarily refreshing and hydrating and offers dry hair the perfect balance. Glycerin will give a deep treatment to dry scalp and dry hair, will define curls and minimize frizz. Keep in mind glycerin must be diluted for best results. This shampoo may not be suitable for those who use permanent hair dye.

Almond oil is packed with vitamins and minerals and is recommended for damage and split ends. Aloe Vera contains enzymes and valuable alkalizing properties that can naturally balance the pH level of your scalp, removing dry, dead cells and promoting hair growth. It also acts to alleviate irritation and itching. Geranium essential oil promotes circulation, has an overall calming effect and adds a pleasant, mild fragrance. Both hair loss and dry, damaged hair can be treated with this shampoo.

Regenerating Cedarwood Oil Conditioner

Ingredients:

- Water (½ cup)
- Olive Oil (½ cup)
- Comfrey Root (a few pieces)

- Herbs (try elderflower and dandelion)
- Cedarwood Essential Oil (5-7 drops)

Directions:

Boil water and allow the comfrey root to steep for 30 minutes. (You may also add any other herbs of your choice.) Strain infusion and pour all ingredients into a container. Shake well until combined. Lather onto your hair, let sit for 5 minutes and rinse well. Gently towel dry.

Benefits:

A nutritive balm for dry hair, it regulates sebum and is packed with nutrients. Its regenerative properties are ideal for anyone, but keep in mind it is a heavier solution, which may be best used regularly if you have very dry hair. One of its most praised benefits is its ability to tame frizzy hair and wild curls. Olive oil adds extra shine and a super silky texture.

Comfrey root treats dry and damaged hair thanks to its high content of Vitamin A, minerals and antioxidants. It also nourishes your hair with large quantities of allantoin, rosmarinic acid and mucilage, which will help stimulate hair growth and brighten dull hair. This herb also has anti-inflammatory and emulsifying properties that can add more body and texture to your hair. Dandelion softens your hair and it makes it thicker and stronger. Its high content of vitamin A promotes hair growth and may surprise you with some natural highlights in your hair. Elderflowers contain astringent properties that can soothe your scalp and stimulate the repair of dry or damaged hair. Cedarwood essential oil will strengthen your hair and add a subtle and refreshing fragrance.

Softening and Hydrating Argan Oil and Thyme Essential Oil Conditioner

Ingredients:

- Argan Oil (3-5 teaspoons)
- Maple Syrup (2-3 teaspoons)
- Thyme Essential Oil (7 drops)

Directions:

Combine and mix all the ingredients until you have a smooth, paste-like consistency. Lather onto your hair, let sit for 5 minutes, and rinse well. Gently towel dry.

Benefits:

This conditioner is more intensive than others, as it contains a combination of highly moisturizing ingredients that act directly to nourish your hair with an oil-heavy base. Argan oil is very rich in Vitamin A, E and antioxidants and can help regenerate and soften hair, giving it extra body and shine. Thyme is great for stimulating circulation, making your hair thick and lustrous and combating irritation. After regular use, damaged hair and split ends will be of no problem and your hair will look and feel strong and healthy.

Hair Masks

Strengthening and Energy-boosting Pumpkin and Sea Buckthorn Oil Mask

Ingredients:

- Olive Oil (2-3 teaspoons)
- Cooked Pumpkin (2-3 slices)
- Sea Buckthorn Essential Oil (5-7 drops)

Directions:

Blitz all ingredients together in your blender (or mash well) until you achieve a creamy consistency. Apply evenly to your hair and let sit for 20 minutes. Rinse well and gently towel dry.

Benefits:

Olive oil will moisturize and nourish your tips, whilst sea buckthorn will energize and revitalize your hair. Pumpkin makes for a great nutrient-rich base for your conditioning mask, given its soft and malleable texture. It is rich in Vitamin A and potassium and it will enhance hair growth when applied to the scalp. This hair mask is packed with vitamin C, A, beta-carotene and minerals which will activate the process of hair repair and replenish and moisturize your hair after regular use.

Refreshing and Tropical Papaya and Rosemary Oil Mask

Ingredients:

- Coconut Milk (½ cup)
- Papaya (2-3 slices)
- Almond Oil (2-3 tablespoons)
- Rosemary Essential Oil (5-7 drops)

Directions:

Blend the coconut milk with the papaya flesh and add the oils. Blitz everything together in your blender until you achieve a creamy consistency. Apply evenly to your hair and let sit for at least 20-25 minutes. Rinse well and gently towel dry.

Benefits:

Papaya is extremely refreshing and aromatic, giving your hair a vitamin and mineral boost. Papain (an enzyme present in papaya) is known for removing dead cells, activating the production of new ones and preventing hair loss. It works great as a nourishing base for your mask thanks to its soft and creamy texture. It helps your hair become stronger and shinier and can also bring out subtle highlights. Almond oil is like 'food' for your hair – perfect for moisturizing and repairing dryness, whilst rosemary oil is soothing and also stimulates hair growth. Use this mask when you need a boost of mental clarity – aromatherapy with rosemary works as an excellent brain and memory invigorator.

CHAPTER 4

Treating Oily Hair

Oily hair can be such a pain, often leaving hair looking flat and lifeless. You may wonder how are you are supposed to use essential oils whilst keeping greasiness in check. Fortunately, there are several home made recipes that can help combat oiliness by ensuring you use the correct quantities in conjunction with all natural, oil-absorbing ingredients.

Shampoo and Conditioner

Purifying Citrus Oil and Cornstarch Shampoo

Ingredients:
- Warm Water (1 cup)
- Baking Soda (1 tablespoon)
- Cornstarch (2 tablespoons)
- Citrus Essential Oil (5 drops)
- Grapefruit Juice (1/3 cup)
- Grapeseed Oil (2-3 teaspoons)

Directions:

Combine all ingredients in a container and shake well before use. Wash hair with a generous amount of the shampoo and rinse well. Gently towel dry. Store in refrigerator and use within 2 weeks.

Benefits:

Citrus based ingredients are the perfect addition to cleansing oily hair, as they regulate sebum production, remove impurities, and nourish hair due to a high content of antioxidants, magnesium, potassium, and folate. Grapefruit juice refreshes your hair and keeps oils under control, whilst its high vitamin content and gentle acidic structure will clean and revitalize your hair and scalp. Cornstarch intensifies the sebum regulation potential of this shampoo, whilst grapeseed oil helps reduce hair loss and provides deep moisture thanks to its omega-3 fatty acids. After a few weeks of regular use, you will notice a reduction in oiliness and the benefits of added strength and shine.

Exfoliating and Cleansing Lemongrass Oil and Strawberry Shampoo

Ingredients:

- Water (1 cup)
- Castile Liquid Soap (½ cup)
- Herbs (watercress and lemongrass)
- Strawberries (2-3)
- Lemongrass Essential Oil (4-5 drops)
- Grapeseed Oil (2-3 teaspoons)

Directions:

Boil water and pour over herbs. Allow to steep for 30 minutes and strain. Using your blender, blitz your fresh strawberries, herbal infusion, lemongrass and grapeseed oil until smooth. Pour into container and shake well after adding liquid soap. Use shampoo within 2 weeks and store in refrigerator.

Benefits:

Strawberries are an antioxidant packed powerhouse and a great addition to your hair care regime being high in magnesium, omega 3 fatty acids and copper. They are also effective in the prevention of hair loss and ideal for oily hair as they offer gentle hydration without negatively affecting your sebum production. Their exfoliating properties remove dead cells and lifeless follicles. Lemongrass regulates oil production, combats greasiness and has a wonderful tonic and astringent effect. Watercress is rich in minerals and helps revitalize your hair. It is also extremely purifying and it combats hair loss thanks to its zinc and biotin content.

Energizing and Astringent Ginger Root and Lavender Oil Conditioner

Ingredients:

- Water (1 cup)
- Lavender (1 handful)
- Black Tea (2 teaspoons of powder)
- Ginger Root (2 pieces)

- Maple Syrup (3 teaspoons)
- Lavender Essential Oil (4-5 drops)

Directions:

Blitz all ingredients in your blender until you achieve a smooth, paste-like consistency. Allow to sit in your hair for a maximum of 5 minutes. Rinse thoroughly and towel dry. Condition your hair once or twice a week with this formula.

Benefits:

This conditioner contains energizing properties of ginger to offer you intensive purification and vitality. Ginger stimulates circulation of the scalp, which can help increase hair growth, and also contains effective antiseptic properties. Black tea is the hidden secret of this conditioner, as it tightens your pores, strengthens the hair shaft and reduces shedding. It also contains tannic acid, which helps reduce the production of excess oil. Lavender will help regulate sebum, soothe your senses and help you de-stress, whilst its anti-inflammatory properties make a great remedy for a sensitive scalp. Maple syrup will hydrate your hair and prevent breakage. The overall effect of this conditioner is cooling and purifying and offers nourishment and gentle hydration, along with the power of astringent properties in black tea. Use this conditioner twice a week for best results.

Balancing Apricot and Cypress Essential Oil Leave-in Conditioner

Ingredients:

- Apple Cider Vinegar (½ cup)
- Apricot Oil (2-3 teaspoons)
- Cypress Essential Oil (4-5 drops)

Directions:

Mix all ingredients until well combined. Apply to damp hair and leave in. (You can also spritz the product into your hair using a spray bottle.) Use once a week or every two weeks for best results.

Benefits:

This formula contains the balancing properties of cypress essential oil and vinegar for the perfect 'oily hair' leave-in conditioner. Vinegar sanitizes, restores and stimulates the hair, while cypress is an effective deterrent of excess oil. It contains apricot oil, a carrier oil light in consistency, which leaves a slightly sweet fragrance. The beauty of this conditioner is its lightness and its simplicity. When you don't want to invest too many ingredients into your hair care, this is the perfect solution. You'll have shine, smoothness, aromatic pleasure and deep purification.

Hair Masks

Purifying Antioxidant Melon and Orange Essential Oil Mask

Ingredients:

- Berries (of your choice, ½ cup)
- Watermelon (1-2 slices)
- Rosehip Oil (2-3 teaspoons)
- Orange Essential Oil (4-5 drops)

Directions:

Blitz everything together in your blender until you achieve a smooth consistency. Evenly apply to your hair and let sit for 20 minutes. Rinse well and gently towel dry.

Benefits: This mask combines antioxidant-rich and purifying berries with the refreshing and nutritive properties of melon – hydrating and packed with Vitamin C to enhance hair growth whilst keeping your scalp clean and balanced. Rosehip oil adds nourishing Vitamin A that will stimulate hair repair. Orange essential oil will add a zesty aroma to the already fresh, sweet fragrance of the formula, and is known to lift your mood and evoke pleasant thoughts.

Strengthening and Balancing Aloe Vera and Clary Sage Oil Mask

Ingredients:

- Aloe Vera Gel (1/3 cup)
- Banana (1)
- Grapeseed Oil (2 teaspoons)
- Clary Sage Essential Oil (4-5 drops)

Directions:

Blitz everything together in your blender (or mash well) until you achieve a smooth consistency. Evenly apply to your hair and let sit for 15-20 minutes. Rinse well and gently towel dry.

Benefit:

Aloe Vera gently hydrates the hair, protects from damage and helps control frizz or 'fly-away' hairs. Banana is a great base for oily hair as it is loaded with vitamins and adds moisture to the hair shaft without leaving greasiness. Grapeseed oil is light in texture and well tolerated by oily hair, making it the perfect carrier oil to dilute your essential oil. Clary sage essential oil combats inflammation and contains astringent and balancing properties. This mask contains an overall purifying and rejuvenating effect.

CHAPTER 5

Other Issues You Can Treat with Homemade Hair Care

Sometimes it's not enough that we have oily or dry hair; we might also suffer from dandruff or the harsh effects of hair dyes and styling products. An accumulation of issues with our hair may make us feel desperate and confused, since we don't know where to begin or what to treat first. Commercial hair care products promise us so much yet leave us feeling frustrated with little results and that's why homemade shampoo, conditioners or masks are so valuable. You can use a variety of healthful ingredients and adjust or alternate them to meet the demands of your hair troubles. Let's see what homemade hair care can do for several issues you may be struggling with.

Anti-dandruff Hair Care

Cleansing and Antiseptic Rosemary and Tea Tree Oil Shampoo

Ingredients:
- Apple Cider Vinegar (1 cup)
- Water (1 cup)

- Rosemary (1 bunch)
- Grapeseed Oil (2-3 teaspoons)
- Tea Tree Essential Oil (6-8 drops)

Directions:

Boil water and steep rosemary until cooled. Strain infused water, add all ingredients into a container and shake well. Wash your hair twice a week with your desired quantity, then rinse well. Gently towel dry.

Benefits:

This shampoo will purify your hair and gradually eliminate dandruff due to the combined properties of vinegar and tea tree oil, which both heal and deeply cleanse the scalp. Both rosemary and grapeseed oil are also effective in combating dandruff by gently adding moisture to the scalp to soothe flakiness and dryness. Tea tree contains high quantities of eucalyptol, a potent antiseptic and antiviral, and also stimulates hair growth by increasing blood flow to the follicles.

Purifying Tonic Jojoba Oil and Peppermint Oil Conditioner

Ingredients:

- Jojoba Oil (½ cup)
- Peppermint Oil (10 drops)
- Maple Syrup (2 teaspoons)

Directions:

Add all ingredients into a suitable container and shake well until combined. Apply to your hair, let sit for at least 5 minutes, then rinse well. Gently towel dry. For best results, use twice a week.

Benefits:

Peppermint is a powerful aid in combatting dandruff by regulating the pH balance of your scalp and is great for normal to oily hair as it regulates sebum production and purifies your scalp. It has a soothing, cooling effect, whilst its refreshing scent will lift your mood. Jojoba oil will add body to your hair with its deeply moisturizing properties, without making it greasy or oily, whilst maple syrup will hydrate your scalp and nourish dry, brittle hair. Peppermint and jojoba accelerate hair growth and stimulate circulation to the scalp. This formula's anti-inflammatory properties are perfect for a sensitive scalp or oily hair.

What about Dyed or Damaged Hair?

Restorative Orange and Almond Oil Shampoo

Ingredients:

- Apple Cider Vinegar (1 cup)
- Baking Soda (1 teaspoon)

- Almond Oil (2-3 teaspoons)
- Orange Essential Oil (10 drops)

Directions:

Add all ingredients into a suitable container and shake well until combined. Apply to your hair, let sit for at least 5 minutes, then rinse well. Gently towel dry. For best results use twice a week.

Benefits:

This shampoo will nourish your hair with an abundance of vitamins and minerals to repair damage from frequent coloring. Almond oil helps repair dry, split ends and its rich moisturizing properties work in harmony with the refreshing and replenishing effects of orange essential oil. This formula deeply cleanses and invigorates, leaving your hair feeling fresh, vibrant and shiny.

Strengthening Argan Oil and Geranium Oil Conditioner

Ingredients:

- Argan Oil (3 teaspoons)
- Coconut Milk (1/3 cup)
- Geranium Essential Oil (10 drops)

Directions:

Add all ingredients into a suitable container and shake well until combined. Apply to your hair, let sit for 5-8 minutes, then rinse well. Gently towel dry. Use weekly to treat split ends and dry, damaged hair.

Benefits:

Argan oil may not be the most cost-effective solution, but its invaluable source of Vitamin E and fatty acids deeply nourish and repair the hair, leaving it shiny and silky. Argan oil, along with coconut milk, makes hair easier to manage and keeps it looking fresh and smooth. It also combats hair loss and damage due to the high concentration of antioxidants. Geranium essential oil strengthens the hair's follicles and shaft and offers a great antioxidant boost to damaged hair with a sweet, rose-like scent. This conditioner is perfect for curly hair so that combing and styling are less problematic.

Effective Products for Hair Growth

Regenerating Nettle and Clary Sage Oil Mask

Ingredients:

- Avocado (1)
- Nettle (2-3 bunches)
- Olive Oil (1/4 cup)
- Clary Sage Oil (10 drops)

Directions:

Boil nettle bunches until they become soft and blitz all ingredients in your blender until you achieve a smooth consistency. Gently massage and apply onto your hair and scalp, and let sit for 15-20 minutes. Rinse well and gently towel dry.

Benefits:

This mask is the perfect remedy if you run the risk of balding or your hair is fine or thinning. Nettle, otherwise known as stinging nettle, is rich in Vitamin A, B, C, D and K and helps stimulates the scalp to encourage new hair growth. Olive oil will offer the added moisture and antioxidants your hair craves, while clary sage will also aid in stimulating the scalp and helps enhance the properties in olive oil and nettle.

Moisturizing Cranberry and Rosemary Oil Mask

Ingredients:

- Cranberries (1 cup)
- Rose Petals (1 handful)
- Coconut Oil (1/4 cup)
- Rosemary Essential Oil (10 drops)

Directions:

Blitz all ingredients together in your blender until you achieve a smooth consistency. Evenly apply to your hair and let sit for 15 minutes. Rinse well and gently towel dry. *Note: You can also steep rose petals in 1 cup boiling water for 30 minutes for a runnier consistency.*

Benefits:

Cranberries are packed full of antioxidants and Vitamin C and have a regenerative effect on your scalp, which can aid in the treatment of hair loss. Rose petals are also rich in Vitamin C, provide natural moisturize and hydration and increase blood flow to the scalp and hair follicles, leaving your hair glossy and soft. Further moisturizing properties come from the coconut oil base, whilst rosemary aids in the growth of new hair with an overall balancing and therapeutic effect. The antiseptic properties in these ingredients make this mask great for oily hair or scalp irritations.

Exotic Turmeric and Ylang-ylang Oil Conditioner

Ingredients:

- Powdered Turmeric (1 teaspoon)
- Coconut Milk (1/4 cup)
- Ylang Ylang Oil (10 drops)

Directions:

Combine and mix all ingredients until you achieve a creamy consistency. Gently massage and apply onto your hair and scalp and let sit for 8 minutes. Rinse well and gently towel dry, ensuring turmeric does not stain your clothes or towels.

Benefits:

Turmeric is a powerful spice with numerous medicinal properties, which is being used by more and more people particularly for its cosmetic purposes. Extremely valued in Middle Eastern cultures and Ayurvedic medicine, it will rejuvenate your hair, soothe your scalp, cure itching and irritation and promote hair growth. Ylang Ylang oil will bring a sweet and exotic fragrance to your hair, whilst it also stimulates hair growth, cures dandruff and works perfectly on regulating oily hair.

Fortifying and Revitalizing Cinnamon and Patchouli Oil Conditioner

Ingredients:
- Powdered Cinnamon (1 teaspoon)
- Coconut Oil (1/3 cup)
- Maple Syrup (3 teaspoons)
- Cedarwood Essential Oil (10 drops)
- Patchouli Essential Oil (10 drops)

Directions:

Combine and mix all ingredients until you achieve a creamy consistency. Gently massage and apply onto your hair and scalp and let sit for 6-8 minutes. Rinse well and gently towel dry.

Benefits:

Cinnamon is fortifying and improves circulation on your scalp to promote hair growth. Maple syrup will deeply hydrate the hair, whilst cedarwood essential oil stimulates the scalp and hair follicles and revitalizes and reduces dryness. Patchouli essential oil adds an alluring and intoxicating scent to this nourishing formula and also helps treat dandruff and oily hair. This conditioner is great for all hair types, particularly oily hair, as it contains astringent properties.

Make Your Hair Shine

Soothing Chamomile Oil and Argan Oil Leave-in Conditioner

Ingredients:
- Apple Cider Vinegar (½ cup)
- Water (½ cup)
- Chamomile (1 bunch or 1 teabag)
- Argan Oil (3 teaspoons)
- Chamomile Essential Oil (10 drops)

Directions:
Boil water and pour over chamomile herbs/tea. Allow to steep until cool, then strain. Add all ingredients into a suitable container (you can use a spray bottle for easy application) and shake well until combined. Apply to your hair and scalp, and leave in.

Benefits:

Vinegar strengthens your hair and makes it bright and shiny, while chamomile combats inflammation and can bring out subtle hues and highlights in your hair, particularly if you are blonde. Chamomile also has a notable soothing and softening effect, leaving you with silky, shiny hair. If your hair is normal to dry, feel free to add a little more moisturizing argan oil, which is extremely effective for its anti-aging properties, too. It promotes cell generation and your hair will grow thicker and healthier after regular application. This leave-in conditioner will give your hair a beautiful, natural sheen.

Hydrating Coconut Oil and Lavender Oil Conditioner

Ingredients:

- Citrus Juice (orange, lemon or grapefruit, ½ cup)
- Coconut Oil (1/3 cup)
- Lavender Oil (10 drops)

Directions:

Add all ingredients into a suitable container and shake well until combined. Apply to your hair and scalp, let sit for 5 minutes, then rinse well. Gently towel dry.

Benefits:

This quick and easy solution for extra shine works best with oily hair due to the astringent and purifying properties of citrus fruit. You can choose lemon or grapefruit if you have too much sebum and your hair gets dull and oily fast. Alternatively, you can opt for orange juice for additional nutrients and a hydrating effect. Coconut oil will soften your hair and make it glossy and silky. Lavender oil is one of the best essential oils for enhancing the properties in this conditioner by adding shine and controlling dandruff.

Tips for Detangling Your Hair

Vinegar and Eucalyptus Oil Spray

Ingredients:

- Water (1 cup)
- Apple Cider Vinegar (2 teaspoons)
- Eucalyptus Essential Oil (5 drops)

Directions:

Add all ingredients into a suitable container (you can use a spray bottle for easy application) and shake well until combined. Apply to your hair and leave in.

Benefits:

This refreshing, light spray will detangle your hair and make brushing and combing so much easier: no more frustrating knots and hair breakage! Vinegar will add strength and shine to your hair. *(Don't worry about any smell, it will disappear quickly.)* Eucalyptus oil is soothing and refreshing with antiseptic properties, aiding in the treatment of flakiness and dandruff.

Coconut Milk and Myrrh Oil Conditioner

Ingredients:

- Coconut Milk (½ cup)
- Argan Oil (2 teaspoons)
- Myrrh Essential Oil (5 -7 drops)

Directions:

Combine and mix all ingredients until you achieve a creamy consistency. Apply to your hair and let sit for 5-7 minutes and gently comb your hair. (Start from the ends and work your way up.) Once hair is detangled, rinse well and gently towel dry.

Benefits:

Coconut milk will help you detangle your hair whilst enriching it with moisture. Argan oil adds a naturally glossy look to your hair while also providing lavish nourishment for your scalp – it is often used alone as a leave-in detangling agent. Another use for this combination is its effectiveness in treating dandruff due to the restorative powers of myrrh essential oil, so don't hesitate to take advantage of this recipe's multifunctional purposes. This formula is great for all hair types, particularly those who have dry or brittle hair.

THANK YOU

Thank you for purchasing this book and exploring the methods and ingredients that will enable you to prepare your very own hair care products at home. I hope that my passion for natural beauty has helped you master a few simple steps in creating the most effective and aromatic hair care products for your personal use.

By simply understanding how each herb, oil, or other ingredient contributes to the health of your hair, you have learnt to tailor each recipe to treat your hair with the most nourishing formula that is most suited to your hair type, whilst indulging your senses in a deeply fulfilling mind and body experience.

Do keep in mind that essential oils and other all-natural ingredients act in a progressive and steady manner. Some solutions require weeks (or even months) of use until your hair starts visibly regenerating, so don't feel discouraged if you don't see immediate results. Shine, smoothness and moisture can be achieved quickly and easily, but getting rid of dandruff, split ends and promoting hair growth and repair may take time with regular maintenance. Feel free to experiment with various hair masks, shampoos and conditioners and stick to what is working best for you for long-term results.

Give your hair the time and the opportunity to heal and regenerate; your diligence and patience will pay off, because you deserve it!

I love keeping in touch with my readers, so stay connected with the *Carma Books* community and email list for more books on holistic and natural health and living. Until next time, I wish you a beautiful journey in happiness and health.

A WORD FROM THE PUBLISHER

Hi, I'm Carmen, a holistic health geek with a passion for health, herbalism, natural remedies, as well as whole-food and plant-based lifestyles. After resolving various health issues I have struggled with for many years, I aim to inspire and help improve your health and longevity by sharing the tireless hours of research and valuable information I have discovered throughout my journey. Through the power of nutrition and lifestyle, with an evidence-based approach, I believe you can achieve your health and wellness goals.

If you enjoyed this book, I would love to hear how it has benefited you and invite you to leave a short review on Amazon - your valuable feed-back is always appreciated!

*You are invited to to join our **Free Book Club** mailing list. Sign up via our website to receive **special offers** and **free for a limited time** Health & Wellness eBooks!*

'A conscious approach to health & wellness'

carmabooks.com

THANK YOU

Printed in Poland
by Amazon Fulfillment
Poland Sp. z o.o., Wrocław